Which Road Next?

by Jonathan Dietrich

Table of Contents

A Lamp for our Journey

"Your word
is a lamp to my feet
and a light to my path."
Psalm 119:105

Imagine with me that your father lives in a village very far from you. He would like you to come visit him, so he writes you a letter telling you how you can get ready and which roads to take. He writes details about which parts of the road are especially dangerous and how to be safe or to avoid certain parts. He also tells you about where to find help along the way and lists some interesting things to see. As you prepare for and embark on your journey, you are happy and feel safe, as long as you carry your father's letter with you.

In reality, your heavenly Father has indeed written you a letter. He loves you and me so much that He wants us to come live with Him. The problem is that the road to heaven is very narrow and straight and not many people know the road. Many wide roads turn to the right and to the left and are well traveled by many people, but these roads are very dangerous. Our heavenly Father wants to make sure that we stay on the right road and do not end up in dangerous place. So He has written a letter to us, to show us the way. The letter is long, but in it are found all the necessary details for your trip. If you read the letter and follow its counsel, you will eventually arrive at your Father's house and can be with Him. Of course, this letter is the Word of God, the Bible.

The good news is that this letter from your Father in heaven is more sure than a letter from your earthly father. Your earthly father may forget some parts of the road or may make a mistake. But your heavenly Father never makes mistakes. His letter to you is perfect. And if you follow step by step what is written, you will be safe.

As you do this, you will be safe because this letter is better than the best *lamp* that was ever made. This one does not blow out in the wind or run out of kerosene. The batteries do not get used up. The light never grows dim. The light is always bright enough to keep you safe on the road. This wonderful *lamp* shows you the dangers in your path and always orients you to stay on the narrow path so that you do not take the wrong path. And in fact, this light grows brighter and brighter the more you use it!

Have you seen this letter from our Father? Do you have a copy of this letter at home? If not, do all in your power to get a copy. Then, read it, study it, obey it! The Bible will become to you your trusted *lamp*, a source of light and safety for your journey through life.

Many Roads

"Thus says the Lord of hosts:
'Consider your ways!' "
(Haggai 1:7)

Perhaps you are wondering, "Why is this Bible lamp so important for me today? I already know about the Bible. Why is it necessary for me to read the Bible more? We have already been taught us about Jesus; what more is there to learn?"

Or, perhaps you believe the often-repeated idea that as long as we all use the same Bible, it doesn't matter exactly what we believe as long as we believe in Jesus. The idea is proposed that as long as we carry our lamp with us, we can each choose one among *many roads* according to our preference and still arrive at the final destination.

One day, while visiting with a friend of mine, we talked about accepting truth and the concept of baptism. He brought up his belief that "since numerous other denominations practice the same baptism (immersion in the name of the Father, Son, and Holy Spirit), all are basically the same." Adding to his case he stated, "All of us Christians are followers of Jesus. We may be on *many roads*, but we are all children of God."

Then, to reinforce his conclusion, he told a short parable about *many roads*. Several people are traveling toward a common destination. One chooses the shorter road, while others each choose one among the *many roads* that are wider and more traveled. Because everybody's destination was the same, they all arrived safely.

This sounds comforting and may help us to calm our troubled consciences when we are under conviction, but is this really what the Bible teaches?

Is it really true...

- ...that as long as we all use the same Bible, we are all walking in the truth?

- ...that as long as we say we believe in Jesus, we are walking on the right path?

- ...that various people on different roads are all children of God?

- ...that there are many paths of truth and that we are free to chose our path of preference and still arrive at our destination?

Let's take a careful look at these four questions.

As long as we all use the same Bible, are we all walking in the truth?

In his second temptation, Satan quoted scripture. He knows Scripture very well, much better than you or I know. Satan said, *"It is written..." (Matthew 4:6)*, thinking that quoting a Bible verse would put Jesus off guard and cause Him to fall under temptation. Jesus replied with, *"It is written...." (Matthew 4:7)* By using Scripture to tempt Jesus, Satan was actually disobeying other Scripture.

Satan will use Scripture anytime it is to his advantage. He does not mind if Scripture is quoted, as long as there is some error mixed in with the truth. Be very careful! Just because a teacher uses Scripture verses does not automatically make his message truthful.

Satan used the same Bible that Jesus used, but for purposes against God's will. He chose a passage that appeared to support his idea, but it was a passage plucked out of context. The Bible is not a magic book that we can carry around to save us. What matters is that we really believe and practice all of what it says.

As long as we say that we believe in Jesus, does that mean we are on the same path?

"Believe on the Lord Jesus Christ, and you will be saved, you and your household." (Acts 16:31)

"He who believes and is baptized will be saved; but he who does not believe will be condemned." (Mark 16:16)

These verses are wonderfully simple and wonderfully true! Eternal life is a free gift (Romans 6:23) given to those who believe. We can do nothing (Ephesians 2:8-9) to earn salvation! But let us be clear about what it means to believe. Believing is more than just an empty repeating of the the words "I believe."

Jesus taught, *"Every tree is known by its fruit." (Luke 6:44)*. And then He asked a very important question. *"But why do you call Me 'Lord, Lord,' and do not <u>do the things which I say</u>?" (Luke 6:46)*

"Not everyone who says to Me, 'Lord, Lord,' shall enter the kingdom of heaven, but he who <u>does the will of My Father</u> in heaven." (Matthew 7:21)

Many, many people who profess to be walking in the right path actually fail to do God's will. They may be very active in the church and respected by many. But by their fruits they demonstrate that their belief in God is really very shallow or non-existent. These people will hear the horrible declaration from Jesus: *"I never knew you; depart from Me, you who practice lawlessness!" (Matthew 7:23)* Jesus does not classify people by their profession, who they claim to be or what path they claim to walk in. What is important to Jesus is not lip service, but heart service. He does not want a do-nothing belief. He wants genuine belief that yields fruit.

Even the demons believe and confess that Jesus is the Son of God, and actually preach elements of the truth! (Mark 1:24; Acts 16:17) But demons are not a source of light; they are darkness. Their belief is lacking an essential ingredient: they do not <u>do</u> the will of God in heaven. They are not obedient to Him.

This missing ingredient is explained in the book of James. Be sure to read the context of these verses in your own Bible.

"What does it profit, my brethren, if someone says he has faith but does not have works? Can faith save him?" (James 2:14)

"Thus also faith by itself, if it does not have works, is dead." (James 2:17)

"You believe that there is one God. You do well. Even the demons believe--and tremble!" (James 2:19)

You see, even Satan and his angels believe. But we would sincerely hope that we are on a different road than the one the devil and his angels are on!

What, then, is the difference between true belief and incomplete belief? In a word, "obedience." Jesus says,

"If you love Me, keep My commandments." (John 14:15)

"For this is the love of God, that we keep His commandments. And His commandments are not burdensome." (1 John 5:3)

Genuine belief in Jesus is always accompanied by a changed life! Genuine belief is accompanied by the abandonment of sin. Genuine belief always results in true obedience—not forced obedience, but obedience that comes from love to God.

Are we all children of God if we walk on different roads?

Genetically, all human beings are children of God since we all descended from Adam who was *"the son of God." (Luke 3:38)* But God is not very interested in our genetics to determine if we are His children! A true child of God, as defined in Scripture, is one who chooses to become a child of God!

"In this the children of God and the children of the devil are manifest: Whoever does not <u>practice righteousness</u> is not of God, nor is he who does not <u>love his brother</u>." (1 John 3:10)

"Those who are the <u>children of the flesh</u>, these are not the children of God; but the children of the promise are counted as the seed." (Romans 9:8)

"For if you live according to the flesh you will die; but if by the Spirit you <u>put to death the deeds of the body</u>, you will live. For as many as are <u>led by the Spirit of God</u>, these are sons of God." (Romans 8:13-14)

"But as many as <u>received Him</u>, to them He gave the right to become children of God, to those who <u>believe in His name</u>: who were born, not of blood, nor of the will of the flesh, nor of the will of man, but of God." (John 1:12-13)

"He who <u>overcomes</u> shall inherit all things, and I will be his God and he shall be My son." (Revelation 21:7)

The good news is that anybody, by God's grace and through His power, can become a child of God if they want to.

I may become a child of God if I...

- ...practice righteousness.
- ...love my brother.
- ...am not controlled by the desires of the flesh.
- ...put to death the deeds of the body.
- ...am led by the Spirit of God.
- ...receive Jesus and believe in His name.
- ...overcome sin in my life.

"Behold what manner of love the Father has bestowed on us, that we should be called children of God!" (1 John 3:1)

There is <u>only one way</u> to become a child of God. I cannot become a child of God on my own. But because of God's great love for me, I may choose to become His child. Through His help and through the power of the Holy Spirit, I may receive Him and believe in His name.

Receiving Him involves more than saying "I believe" with your lips. Receiving Jesus also means receiving the Word, because Jesus is the Word. (John 1:1) What does it mean to receive the Word?

"But he who <u>received</u> seed on the good ground is he who <u>hears</u> the word and <u>understands</u> it, who indeed <u>bears fruit</u> and <u>produces</u>: some a hundredfold, some sixty, some thirty." (Matthew 13:23)

"The seed is the Word of God." (Luke 8:11)

Receiving the word means to:

- …hear the Word
- …understand the Word
- …produce fruit

In other words, receiving Jesus means being transformed by Him and His Word. *Many roads* are full of hypocrites who claim to be God's children, but their claims are empty. Perhaps they hear the Word of God, but stop there without striving for and understanding. Or perhaps they understand, but refuse to produce fruit. They are hypocrites, untransformed, and fruitless. They say "I believe" but they have not truly received the Word or been transformed by it. They are like empty wells, claiming to have the water of life, but actually dry.

Seeing hypocrites in the church can make us feel like abandoning the truth. It is not fair that people should claim to be God's children and then act like the devil's children. But we must never be distracted by other people. Our job is not to study the hypocrites. A hypocrite is powerless to change the truth. The truth never changes. We choose to not follow hypocrites, but to follow the truth.

If you wish to follow the road of truth, take care to study the truth and practice it. Following those who merely claim to be God's children will surely lead us along a dangerous path.

"My little children, let us not love in word or in tongue, but <u>in deed</u> and <u>in truth</u>. And <u>by this we know that we are of the truth</u>, and shall assure our hearts before Him." (1 John 3:18-19)

Are there many paths of truth that we are free to choose according to our personal preference and still arrive at our destination?

Along our journey, we will encounter *many roads*. Many of them are attractive to us and appeal to our natural desires. We often prefer to take the easy roads. But friends, these roads are not really easy.

The only common destination for the *many roads* is destruction and death!

"There is a way that seems right to a man, but its end is the way of death." (Proverbs 14:12)

It is very dangerous for us to choose the way that *"seems right"* to us. We cannot trust our own judgment, our own ideas, our personal preferences, no matter how right they seem to be. We cannot be safe merely preferring that path that our family is on. We cannot be safe merely preferring the path of our favorite teacher. We are only safe as we use the lamp, the Bible, to give us light and guidance through life's way.

Perhaps it *"seems right"* to you to not associate yourself with those who claim to walk in the truth, but are obviously hypocrites. Hypocrites come and go, but truth remains. Scripture warns us, *"Many will follow their destructive ways, because of whom the way of truth will be blasphemed." (2 Peter 2:2)* Don't let the hypocrites lead you on to destruction with them!

Perhaps it *"seems right"* to you to follow the example of your parents, who were good people and followed what light that they knew. For you to do otherwise would seem like a rejection of your parents. But in doing what seems right to you rather than what is right before God, you are rejecting additional light and truth that God is revealing to you.

Or perhaps it *"seems right"* to faithfully follow your pastor who was well-trained on how to study and interpret Scripture. Perhaps you feel that many Bible verses are so complicated that it is best to leave their interpretation to a trained pastor. But by neglecting personal study of God's Word, you are missing out on discovering truth for yourself.

14

No, it is not safe to consult our preferences in choosing a road that *"seems right"* among *many roads*.

"Jesus said to him, 'I am the way, the truth, and the life. No one comes to the Father except through Me.' " (John 14:6)

Jesus is the way; there is only one way that is the right way. Jesus is the truth; there is only one truth that exists, not several. Jesus is the life; there is only one life eternal, and that is a gift that comes from God for those who believe.

What will you choose today? Will you choose to follow your inclinations and preferences and thus follow one of the *many roads* to destruction? Or will you choose to receive the Word, practice it, and walk in the way, the truth, and the life? I pray that you will choose Jesus and His Word as your only authority as you search for the path of truth.

"In all your ways acknowledge Him, and He shall direct your paths." (Proverbs 3:6)

Further study

Job 8:11-15

The Broad Path

"Enter by the narrow gate;
for wide is the gate
and broad is the way
that leads to destruction,
and there are many who go in by it."
(Matthew 7:13)

Why is the road to destruction so broad?

It is broad because so many people have chosen to walk this road. This *broad path* is the road of the majority, the road well traveled. *"There are many who go in by it."*

Why do so many people walk in this *broad path*?

- This path is easy to find, even in the dark. In fact, we don't even have to look for it. It is the path of least resistance. The path seems easy and smooth as it slopes gently downward.

- Walking in this path feels natural because in it, we can fulfill our natural desires. In this path we are not required to renounce every evil desire.

- The path is popular, crowded with a great number of people including professed Christians, people who claim to know God. The path seems right to them since it is so popular. They reason that surely, all these other people wouldn't have chosen the wrong path. They base their decision on silly,

16

circular logic: "I will join the many people who use this path because many people use this path."

- People do not stop to carefully consider where they are headed. They do not realize that the sure destination of the *broad path* is destruction.

This path is full of people with good intentions. It is full of people who think they will be saved. It is full of baptized Christians who faithfully attend church and who even might sing in the choir.

How could I be found to be walking in the broad path?

I may walk in the *broad path* by doing anything contrary to the Ten Commandments, the Law of God. The *broad path* presents to me numerous options and variations to do wrong, and I may walk in the *broad path* by choosing any one of them.

I may also choose to walk in the *broad path* by refusing the light. I may learn and understand a clear teaching in Scripture, but decide to reject it in favor of a human tradition. Rejecting light and truth is always dangerous, as it assures that I will stay on the path of darkness.

Two categories of people walk on the *broad path:* pagans and hypocrites. The pagans do not claim to walk in the path of truth. But the hypocrites claim to walk in the path of truth while remaining on the *broad path.* The hypocrites are generally divided into two sub-categories: smooth teachers and people with itching ears.

What is the final destination of the *broad path*?

"...the way that leads to <u>destruction</u>..." (Matthew 7:13)

"There is a way that seems right to a man, but its end is the way of <u>death</u>." (Proverbs 16:25)

"The paths of their way turn aside, they go nowhere and <u>perish</u>." (Job 6:18)

We cannot safely choose a way that *"seems right"* to us, even if that way is broad and popular. The Word of God must be our only sure guide in life. Unfortunately, many people choose smooth teachers as their guides.

Smooth Teachers

"O My people!
Those who lead you
cause you to err,
and destroy the way of your paths."
(Isaiah 3:12)

It is a sad fact today that many leaders are leading the people in the broad way. The leaders set before the people an example by walking in the broad way and multitudes of people are following them. Sometimes, the leader is ignorant that he is in the broad path. But astonishingly, many leaders choose to close their eyes and march onward blindly, knowing that they are rejecting truth. Some things *"they willfully forget." (2 Peter 3:5)*

Why would a teacher be so cruel as to lead so many people astray? What would motivate him to commit such a crime? A teacher of the Word of God should be *"a guide to the blind, a light to those who are in darkness." (Romans 2:19)* But *"Can the blind lead the blind? Will they not both fall into the ditch?" (Luke 6:39)*

[[picture of blind leading blind]]

Some *smooth teachers* hide the truth because they fear that if they were to faithfully preach the Word of God, they would lose their salary. People give offerings to the teacher or preacher because they like him. And if he teaches things they don't like, they might stop supporting him financially.

So the *smooth teachers* exchange eternal riches in heaven and favor with God for a few pennies on earth and favor with man on the broad path.

Some *smooth teachers* hide the truth because they fear for their reputation. Perhaps their friends and family that they have taught over the years might mock them and call them fools. Perhaps friends and family would even abandon them. So the *smooth teachers* choose to exchange the fear of God for fear of the people on the broad path.

Some *smooth teachers* hide the truth because they do not want to be embarrassed. One who has taught error for ten or thirty or even fifty years would be forced to admit that he was wrong all those years if he started preaching the truth. That might be humiliating and embarrassing. So the *smooth teachers*, instead of bringing glory and honor to God by accepting the light of truth as it shines on them, choose to cultivate their own pride and honor among those in the broad path.

Are you a *smooth teacher*? I hope not. Do you know some passages of truth but choose to "willfully forget" them when you talk with people? Or are you one who simply repeats what he has been taught without personally confirming and verifying the teaching in the Bible? Do you have a knowledge of the lamp of the Word of God but sometimes choose to hide it from others and keep them in darkness? If so, unfortunately you are a *smooth teacher*!

"Whoever causes one of these little ones who believe in Me to sin, it would be better for him if a millstone were hung around

his neck, and he were drowned in the depth of the sea."
(Matthew 18:6)

If you are tempted to be a *smooth teacher*, consider the examples of Paul, Peter, and Jeremiah, and others.

Paul was not a *smooth teacher*. He said, *"I am not ashamed of the gospel of Christ." (Romans 1:16) "For I have not shunned to declare to you the whole counsel of God." (Acts 20:27)* He understood that as a teacher of the Word of God, he must faithfully preach the <u>whole</u> message, not just the parts that are smooth or pleasing. Paul warned the shepherds (teachers and preachers) to be faithful in their work, because wolves (false teachers) would come in to attack the sheep (church members). *"So now, brethren, I commend you to God and to the word of His grace, which is able to build you up and give you an inheritance among all those who are sanctified." (Acts 20 32)* Paul was not in the broad path.

Peter was not a *smooth teacher*. His message was not popular, even with the leaders of the church. When confronted by the church leaders who were angered by his straightforward method of preaching the truth, Peter replied, *"We ought to obey God rather than men." (Acts 5:29)* He recognized the important truth that we should not live our lives according to what others are doing, but according to what we ought to do as detailed in God's Word. Peter was not in the broad path.

Jeremiah was not a *smooth teacher*, although he was tempted to be one. He was given a message from God to give to the people. This message was not a popular message, and the people laughed at him and made fun of him. He wanted to hide the message of truth, but found that he could not! Jeremiah remembers his experience here: *"O Lord, You induced me, and I was persuaded; You are stronger than I, and have prevailed. I am in derision daily; everyone mocks me. For when I spoke, I cried out; I shouted, 'Violence and plunder!' Because the word of the Lord was made to me a reproach and a derision daily. Then I said, 'I will not make mention of Him, nor speak anymore in His name.' But His word was in my heart like a burning fire shut up in my bones; I was weary of holding it back, and I could not."* (Jeremiah 20:7-9) Jeremiah could not hold back the truth. He was not in the broad path.

Many churches today are guilty of the sin of *smooth teaching*. If Jesus was here today, He would say as He did to the church leaders in His day, *"Are you not therefore mistaken, because you do not know the Scriptures nor the power of God?"* (Mark 12:24) *"And in vain they worship Me, teaching as doctrines the commandments of men."* (Mark 7:7)

If you are a *smooth teacher*, today can be your last day. Quit your job! Abandon it! Today, chose a new profession: a truth teacher. Make a commitment today to teach only truth untainted with error!

"Preach the word! Be ready in season and out of season. Convince, rebuke, exhort, with all longsuffering and teaching." (2 Timothy 4:2)

You don't have to be blindly leading the blind. You don't have to have a millstone hung around your neck and be sunk to the bottom of the sea. Instead, you can have all your sins cast *"into the depths of the sea." (Micah 7:19)*

You don't have to depend on the dim beams of light coming from tradition. Today, you can choose the Bible as your bright and shining lamp, your only lamp, to guide you through the difficult way of life! No other lamp is comparable in brightness and reliability.

How may I avoid being a *smooth teacher*?

- I will teach the Word of God purely as it is, without mixing false teachings or traditions of men, no matter how widespread they are believed.

- I will choose to open my eyes and search for truth to understand it, and make a commitment to share all truth that I learn with others instead of hiding parts of it from them.

- I will choose to do what I ought to do (obey God) rather than to do what is popular (obey man).

Further study

Isaiah 9:6

Ezechiel 3:17-18

Ezechiel 33:7-8

Ezechiel 34

Proverbs 28:10

Itching Ears

"Woe to the rebellious children," says the Lord,
"who take counsel, but not of Me,
and who devise plans, but not of My Spirit,
that they may add sin to sin."
(Isaiah 30:1)

The soothing teachers who hide truth and light from the people are not the only problem! Often it is the multitudes who do not insist on hearing the truth. Like their teachers, they prefer not to hear the truth. The plain truth makes them uncomfortable. They have *itching ears* to hear things that are pleasing to them and their natural desires. They like the smooth things taught by the smooth teachers.

"This is a rebellious people, lying children, children who will not hear the law of the Lord; who say to the seers, 'Do not see,' and to the prophets, 'Do not prophesy to us right things; speak to us smooth things, prophesy deceits. Get out of the way, turn aside from the path, cause the Holy One of Israel to cease from before us.' " (Isaiah 30:9-11)

Why are the rebellious people called lying children?

These people profess to be God's children, yet are actually annoyed by truth. They want to hear certain things and do not want to hear certain other things. Eventually, they are deceived enough to wish that God would go away from them and leave them alone!

And so they search for their favorite teacher or pastor, who they know will scratch their *itching ears* and speak pleasing things and not worry them too much about such concerning topics as sin, God's Law, and the judgment. These people claim to be in the path of truth, but in reality are walking along the broad road.

Like pain in the eyes of a tired man who awakes from sleep in a dark room to go out into the sunshine, so is the truth to a person who is not accustomed to truth. Jesus is light. (John 8:12) God's Word is light. (Psalms 119:105) Truth is light. (John 3:21) And those who love darkness prefer to avoid the light and remain in darkness. I hope you are not one who loves darkness!

"In [Jesus] was life, and the life was the light of men. And the light shines in the darkness, and the darkness did not comprehend it. That was the true Light *which gives light* to every man *coming into the world. He was in the world, and the world was made through Him, and the world did not know Him."* (John 1:4-5,9-10)

How many people have access to the light?

The true Light (Jesus) gives light to everyone in the world. Nobody is obligated to remain in the darkness. Jesus is Light enough for all.

Why do people love darkness rather than light?

We find the answer a couple of chapters later: *"And this is the condemnation, that the light has come into the world, and men loved darkness rather than light,* because their deeds were evil.*" (John 3:19)* Evildoers hate light. Criminals usually prefer to work at night so their evil deeds are not detected. For a person who loves darkness, light and truth do not scratch their *itching ears* in a way that is pleasing to them.

How is it possible for a person to hate something that is good? How can a person love darkness when there is light available?

Darkness is our natural condition. Left to ourselves, we are full of darkness. Yet God, Who *"commanded light to shine out of darkness... has shone in our hearts." (2 Corinthians 4:6)* He wants us to have light.

But some of us have dull hearts. Something that is dull is not bright. We lack light, not because there is no light, but because we rejected it. Our ears could hear, but we have plugged them. Our eyes could see, but we have blinded them.

"For the hearts of this people have grown dull. Their ears are hard of hearing, and their eyes they have closed, lest they should see with their eyes and hear with their ears, lest they should understand with their hearts and turn, so that I should heal them." (Acts 28:27)

Simply put, a person hates that which is good because he loves that which is evil.

Why do the people reject true doctrine?

"For the time will come when they will not endure sound doctrine, but according to their own desires, because they have itching ears, they will heap up for themselves teachers; and they will turn their ears away from the truth, and be turned aside to fables." (2 Timothy 4:3-4)

Especially at the end of time, people reject true doctrine because they have not conquered their own desires. Perhaps God's Word has commanded you to do something, but you do not feel like obeying. Perhaps God's Word has commanded you not to do something, but you do it anyway because it feels good or it tastes good or it looks good.

Sadly, many people cultivate *itching ears*. They are ruled by their own natural desires and not by the Holy Spirit. They choose for themselves teachers who will satisfy their own desires by scratching their *itching ears* for them. At the same time, they turn their ears away from the truth.

How may I avoid having *itching ears*?

- I will ask God to change my natural desires to become good desires, and to turn my ears toward the truth, not away from it.

- I will search for counsel first from God in His Word, always treating His counsel as the first and best and authoritative above any other counsel or teaching.

- I will accept the light when it shines on me and follow where it leads. I will obey and not ignore God's Word.

Thankfully, I do not have to remain on the broad path with the smooth teachers and with the itching ear people. I can choose to walk on the narrow path!

The Narrow Path

"Because narrow is the gate
and difficult is the way
which leads to life,
and there are few who find it."
(Matthew 7:14)

Why is the road to eternal life so narrow?

The road is narrow because so few people have chosen to walk this road. This *narrow path* is the road of the minority, a road nearly neglected. *"There are few who find it."*

Why do so few people walk in this *narrow path*?

- Everyone is given light enough to direct them toward the *narrow path*, but many refuse to follow the light. To find this path requires effort; we must search for it. The path is difficult and rough in places as it climbs steadily uphill.

- Walking in this path requires self-denial and sacrifice; it requires us to starve our natural desires (all of them), not fulfill them. Pride is not allowed on this path.

- This path is unpopular and can seem lonely at times. People prefer to stay on the wide path with their family or their friends rather than travel the difficult path, sometimes alone.

What does it mean for me to walk in the *narrow path*?

Walking in the *narrow path* means that I do not just profess to be a disciple of Jesus. It means that I practice what I profess. I am in the *narrow path* as I obediently follow <u>everything</u> He as asked me to do, including obeying <u>all</u> of God's Ten Commandments. Jesus said, *"If you want to enter into life, keep the commandments." Matthew 19:17*

"If we say that we have fellowship with Him, and walk in darkness, we lie and do not practice the truth. But if we walk in the light as He is in the light, we have fellowship with one another, and the blood of Jesus Christ His Son cleanses us from all sin." (1 John 1:6-7)

"Now by this we know that we know Him, if we keep His commandments. He who says, 'I know Him,' and does not keep His commandments, is a liar, and the truth is not in him." (1 John 2:3-4)

What is the final destination of the *narrow path*?

"...the way which leads to <u>life</u>..." (Matthew 7:14)

"The way of life winds <u>upward</u> for the wise, that he may turn away from hell below." (Proverbs 15:24)

"In the way of righteousness is <u>life</u>, and in its pathway there is <u>no death</u>." (Proverbs 12:28)

"And the world is passing away, and the lust of it; but he who does the will of God <u>abides forever</u>." (1 John 2:17)

Who does the narrow gate represent?

<u>Jesus</u> says, *"I am the door. If anyone enters by Me, he will be saved, and will go in and out and find pasture." (John 10:9)*

Notice how many doors are mentioned. Jesus is <u>the</u> door, the <u>one</u> door to salvation.

Who does the *narrow path* represent?

The narrow way represents the one unique way of truth. Jesus is the truth.

<u>Jesus</u> says, *"I am the way, the truth, and the life. No one comes to the Father except through Me." (John 14:6)* Who is at the center of this verse? It is Jesus. He is three things here: the Way, the Truth, and the Life. It is through Jesus and Jesus only that we may find eternal life.

Notice that there is one true way, not many. Only one truth exists, not many. There is only one life that is eternal —eternal life through Jesus.

"Then Jesus said to them, 'A little while longer the light is with you. Walk while you have the light, lest darkness overtake you; he who walks in darkness does not know where he is going.' " (John 12:35)

Are there joys along this path?

"You will show me the path of life; in Your presence is fullness of joy; at Your right hand are pleasures forevermore." (Psalm 16:11)

"I have come that they may have life, and that they may have it more abundantly." (John 10:10)

What are some of the challenges of walking the *narrow path*?

- I cannot walk the *narrow path* on my own, *"because the carnal mind is enmity against God; for it is not*

30

subject to the law of God, nor indeed can be. So then, those who are in the flesh cannot please God." *(Romans 8:7-8)* I need a miracle to convert my carnal mind.

- I cannot walk the *narrow path* without a growing, living faith. *"Without faith it is impossible to please Him." (Hebrews 11:6)*

- The path is narrow. There is no room for my own ideas, my own baggage. I must leave behind *"the cares of this world and the deceitfulness of riches." (Mark 4:19)*

To walk this *narrow path* successfully, we need supernatural strength and help. We need our lamp, the Word of God to show us the way. And we need to pass through the narrow gate, stay in the truth, stay in the narrow path. In other words, we need to stay in Jesus.

Further study

Luke 13:23-27

Psalm 25:10

Isaiah 26:7

In Jesus

"As you have therefore
received Christ Jesus the Lord,
so walk in Him, rooted and built up in Him...
You are complete in Him."
(Colossians 2:6-7,10)

Many people desire to walk on the narrow path. They would like to have eternal life and experience Paradise. But sadly, many who begin the narrow path never reach their goal. A temptation distracts them or they loose their focus on Jesus and they slip off the narrow path and find themselves again in darkness on the broad path. How discouraging this can be!

But we need not be discouraged! God has prepared everything that we need to navigate the narrow path. He *"is able to keep you from stumbling." (Jude 1:24)* Do you remember what the narrow gate and the narrow path represent? That's right, they both represent Jesus. As long as we stay *in Jesus*, we are secure on the narrow path to eternal life!

We do not have to worry about falling off the path as long as we keep our eyes on Jesus. *"Looking unto Jesus, the author and finisher of our faith," (Hebrews 12:2)* we may be assured that Jesus will be with us not only at the beginning, but all the way through the destination! The key is to look to Jesus.

How may I walk this narrow path with success?

The only solution is *in Jesus*. Countless souls have begun the journey, desiring to finish, and trying their best. But they have failed in this because their best is not enough! If they would only trust *in Jesus*, they would be sure of success!

To thoroughly study what it means to be *in Jesus* would take far more space than we can afford in this booklet. May the following collection of verses guide you to look to Jesus and encourage you to launch into a deeper study on this topic!

Complete *in Jesus*

"You are complete <u>in Him</u>, who is the head of all principality and power." (Colossians 2:10)

Being complete in Jesus means that in Him, we lack nothing that we need. It is important to note that we are complete <u>in Him</u>, not in some other source. If we are not complete, we must not be in Him. Jesus is the source for all that we need in our journey along the narrow path.

TRUSTING IN JESUS

Faith *in Jesus*

"And be found in Him, not having my own righteousness, which is from the law, but that which is through faith <u>in Christ</u>, the righteousness which is from God by faith." (Philippians 3:9)

(See also: Ephesians 3:12; Galatians 2:16)

Believe *in Jesus*

"For God so loved the world that He gave His only begotten Son, that whoever believes <u>in Him</u> should not perish but have everlasting life." (John 3:16)

"Most assuredly, I say to you, he who hears My word and believes <u>in Him</u> who sent Me has everlasting life, and shall not come into judgment, but has passed from death into life." (John 5:24)

Confidence *in Jesus*

"Now this is the confidence that we have <u>in Him</u>, that if we ask anything according to His will, He hears us." (1 John 5:14)

LIFE IN JESUS

Abide *in Jesus*

"I can of Myself do nothing." (John 5:30)

"Abide <u>in Me</u>, and I in you. As the branch cannot bear fruit of itself, unless it abides in the vine, neither can you, unless you abide in Me. I am the vine, you are the branches. He who abides <u>in Me</u>, and I in him, bears much fruit; for without Me you can do nothing." (John 15:4-5)

(See also: Philippians 3:9; 1 John 2:5-6; 3:24; 4:13)

My best effort is not enough to stay on the narrow path. I can do nothing of myself. But if I abide in Jesus, He will abide in me. My goals become His goals. My life comes from His life. As long as I abide in Jesus and remain connected to Him throughout each day, I cannot fall from the narrow path.

Alive *in Jesus*

"I have been crucified with Christ; it is no longer I who live, but Christ lives in me; and the life which I now live in the flesh I live by faith in the Son of God, who loved me and gave Himself for me." (Galatians 2:20)

"Likewise you also, reckon yourselves to be dead indeed to sin, but alive to God in Christ Jesus our Lord." (Romans 6:11)

(See also: Romans 6:23; 1 Corinthians 15:22; 2 Timothy 1:1)

By default, being alive in Jesus means being dead to sin. To become dead to sin, I give Jesus the permission to remove my desires for sin.

GROWING IN JESUS

Redemption and forgiveness of sins *in Jesus*

"In Him we have redemption through His blood, the forgiveness of sins, according to the riches of His grace." (Ephesians 1:7)

New Creation *in Jesus*

"Therefore, if anyone is in Christ, he is a new creation; old things have passed away; behold, all things have become new." (2 Corinthians 5:17)

(See also: Galatians 6:15)

Walk *in Jesus*

"As you have therefore received Christ Jesus the Lord, so walk in Him." (Colossians 2:6)

Walking in Him means walking in the narrow path.

Be weak *in Jesus*

"And He said to me, 'My grace is sufficient for you, for My strength is made perfect in weakness.' Therefore most gladly I will rather boast in my infirmities, that the power of Christ may rest upon me. Therefore I take pleasure in infirmities, in reproaches, in needs, in persecutions, in distresses, for Christ's sake. For when I am weak, then I am strong."
(2 Corinthians 12:9- 10)

"For though He was crucified in weakness, yet He lives by the power of God. For we also are weak in Him, but we shall live with Him by the power of God toward you." (2 Corinthians 13:4)

No condemnation *in Jesus*

"There is therefore now no condemnation to those who are in Christ Jesus, who do not walk according to the flesh, but according to the Spirit." (Romans 8:1)

Rooted and built up *in Jesus*

"Rooted and built up in Him and established in the faith, as you have been taught, abounding in it with thanksgiving."
(Colossians 2:7)

Established *in Christ*

"Now He who establishes us with you in Christ and has anointed us is God." (2 Corinthians 1:21)

Created *in Christ* for good works

"For we are His workmanship, created in Christ Jesus for good works, which God prepared beforehand that we should walk in them."(Ephesians 2:10)

Sanctified *in Jesus*

"To the church of God which is at Corinth, to those who are sanctified <u>in Christ Jesus</u>, called to be saints, with all who in every place call on the name of Jesus Christ our Lord, both theirs and ours." (1 Corinthians 1:2)

Perfect *in Christ*

"Him we preach, warning every man and teaching every man in all wisdom, that we may present every man perfect <u>in Christ Jesus</u>." (Colossians 1:28)

Preserved *in Jesus*

"Jude, a bondservant of Jesus Christ, and brother of James, To those who are called, sanctified by God the Father, and preserved <u>in Jesus Christ</u>." (Jude 1:1)

FAMILY IN JESUS

Babes *in Christ*

"And I, brethren, could not speak to you as to spiritual people but as to carnal, as to babes <u>in Christ</u>." (1 Corinthians 3:1)

One body/united *in Jesus*

"So we, being many, are one body <u>in Christ</u>, and individually members of one another." (Romans 12:5)

"There is neither Jew nor Greek, there is neither slave nor free, there is neither male nor female; for you are all one <u>in Christ Jesus</u>." (Galatians 3:28)

Sons of God through faith *in Jesus*

"For you are all sons of God through faith <u>in Christ Jesus</u>."
(Galatians 3:26)

Brothers *in Christ*

"To the saints and faithful brethren <u>in Christ</u> who are in Colosse: Grace to you and peace from God our Father and the Lord Jesus Christ." (Colossians 1:2)

Summary

Choosing to walk *in Jesus* on the narrow path of life is a wonderful decision. Although we will surely encounter difficulties and trials, we will also discover joy and satisfaction like we never experienced before.

"You will show me the path of life; in Your presence is fullness of joy; at Your right hand are pleasures forevermore." (Psalm 16:11)

But if we are on the narrow path, we must not forget that there are others still on the broad path who may decide to join the narrow path.

It is the responsibility of all who have light to share that light with others and to encourage them to turn from the darkness of death to the light of life.

The Other Sheep

"Other sheep I have which are not of this fold;
them also I must bring,
and they will hear My voice;
and there will be one flock and one shepherd."
(John 10:16)

Jesus, our Example, came *"to seek and to save that which was lost." (Luke 19:10)* To help us understand the importance of seeking the lost, he told a parable about sheep. Ninety-nine of the one-hundred sheep were safe in the fold. The *other sheep* was outside, lost.

"What man of you, having a hundred sheep, if he loses one of them, does not leave the ninety-nine in the wilderness, and go after the one which is lost until he finds it? And when he has found it, he lays it on his shoulders, rejoicing. And when he comes home, he calls together his friends and neighbors, saying to them, 'Rejoice with me, for I have found my sheep which was lost!' " (Luke 15:4-6)

Who does the shepherd represent?

Jesus says, *"I am the good shepherd." (John 10:14)* Jesus is the Shepherd. He is the Good Shepherd—not just <u>a</u> good shepherd, but <u>the</u> Good Shepherd.

Who are the sheep?

"Know that the Lord, He is God; it is He who has made us, and not we ourselves; we are His people and the sheep of His pasture." (Psalm 100:3) We are the sheep. When I say, *"The*

Lord is my shepherd." (Psalm 23:1), I choose to be one of Jesus' sheep and to follow Him.

But not all sheep are in Jesus' flock; not all sheep are following Him. Many claim "the Lord is my Shepherd," but are not really following Him. Sometimes, the sheep are lost on the broad path because of smooth teachers.

"My people have been lost sheep. Their shepherds have led them astray." (Jeremiah 50:6) " 'Woe to the shepherds who destroy and scatter the sheep of My pasture!' says the Lord." (Jeremiah 23:1)

Other times, it is those people with itching ears who choose the broad path.

How many sheep have gone astray?

"All we like sheep have gone astray; we have turned, every one, to his own way; and the Lord has laid on Him the iniquity of us all." (Isaiah 53:6)

All of us sheep have gone astray. Before we are too hard on the *other sheep* that are not in the fold, let us never forget that we have all been lost, out of the fold, astray.

Where has each lost sheep gone?

Each one turned. To turn means to change direction. Those who remain on the narrow path do not change direction, because the narrow path is straight and upward. By turning astray, the sheep fall from the narrow path and do not remain in Jesus. Each one turned, but not all in the same direction.

Each one turned to his own way. To follow your own way, no matter which direction you are headed, no matter how secure your path seems at the moment, is sure disaster. *"The way of a fool is right in his own eyes."* *(Proverbs 12:15) "There is a way that seems right to a man, but its end is the way of death." (Proverbs 14:12) "Therefore they shall eat the fruit of their own way." (Proverbs 1:31)*

Those sheep who each turn to their own way refuse to listen to the Shepherd Who is the narrow way. These sheep can never be truly safe. They can never find true peace. They can never be secure, as long as they are in their own way. But thankfully, lost sheep can return and find safety, peace, and security in listening to the Shepherd.

"But whoever listens to me will dwell safely, and will be secure, without fear of evil." (Proverbs 1:33)

"For you were like sheep going astray, but have now returned to the Shepherd and Overseer of your souls." (1 Peter 2:25)

Listening to the Shepherd is an important skill to develop, because this is an essential characteristic that differentiates two types of sheep. There are some sheep who have returned to the Shepherd and there are *other sheep* who have gone astray. Let's learn how to classify sheep, so we can determine which category we are in. (You will find it interesting to study John chapter 10. For now, we will select a few verses from this chapter to summarize.)

"He who enters by the door is the shepherd of the sheep. To him the doorkeeper opens, and the sheep hear his voice; and he calls

his own sheep by name and leads them out. And when he brings out his own sheep, he goes before them; and the sheep follow him, for they know his voice." (John 10:2-4)

"I am the good shepherd; and I know My sheep, and am known by My own." (John 10:14)

Before continuing, let's notice a few important points.

When the Shepherd comes to the door, how do the sheep know it is Him?

They hear His voice because they are listening for Him. They know His voice because they recognize it.

Where is the Shepherd in relation to the sheep?

The Shepherd is before the sheep, and the sheep follow him. We can face any trial before us knowing that Jesus our Shepherd has already gone before us and will help us through the difficulty.

Why do the sheep follow Him?

They follow Him because they know His voice. They are accustomed to it. They hear it every day. Jesus' sheep listen to Him daily, continually.

"Yet they will by no means follow a stranger, but will flee from him, for they do not know the voice of strangers." (John 10:5)

When the stranger comes to the door, how do the sheep know it is a stranger?

The sheep do not recognize the voice of strangers. Jesus' sheep know no other voice than His voice. They do not give entrance to those who teach contrary to the truth.

Jesus goes on to give further details in His parable.

"And other sheep I have which are not of this fold; them also I must bring, and they will hear My voice; and there will be one flock and one shepherd." (John 10:16)

Here, Jesus talks about the *other sheep*. These sheep *"are not of this fold."* They do not yet hear his voice, but apparently some of the sheep outside the fold *"will hear"* His voice sometime in the future.

How many flocks of sheep will there be following Jesus?

Only one.

How many true shepherds will there be?

Only one.

Notice that Jesus did not say that the *other sheep* can follow Him while remaining in the other flocks. There is only one true Shepherd and only one genuine flock traveling the narrow path. All other flocks are following false shepherds and traveling the broad path. They have itching ears and are following smooth teachers, or are not even interested in the truth at all.

Jesus said, *"them also I must bring."* He didn't say, "them also may stay where they are." No, no! *"The Lord is not slack concerning His promise, as some count slackness, but is longsuffering toward us, not willing that any should perish but that all should come to repentance." (2 Peter 3:9)* He earnestly and tenderly calls the *other sheep* to listen to His voice and to come and follow Him.

"Therefore 'Come out from among them and be separate, says the Lord. Do not touch what is unclean, and I will receive you.' " (2 Corinthians 6:17)

How can we identify Jesus' sheep?

"Jesus answered them, 'I told you, and you do not believe. The works that I do in My Father's name, they bear witness of Me. But you do not believe, because you are not of My sheep, as I said to you. My sheep hear My voice, and I know them, and they follow Me. And I give them eternal life, and they shall never perish; neither shall anyone snatch them out of My hand. My Father, who has given them to Me, is greater than all; and no one is able to snatch them out of My Father's hand. I and My Father are one.' " (John 10:25-30)

We can identify Jesus' sheep in three points from this passage:

- Jesus' sheep believe in Him.
- Jesus' sheep hear His voice.
- Jesus' sheep follow Him.

In which flock are you?

Jesus cannot be before you if you are walking in the broad path of error. If you know the truth but refuse to walk in it, you are rejecting Jesus as your Good Shepherd by refusing to listen to Him. You are choosing to walk with the other flocks heading to destruction.

But you do not have to remain one of the *other sheep;* you can switch flocks! You can choose today to have Jesus before you and to walk on the narrow path. You can choose the Good Shepherd as your Shepherd by choosing to listen to His voice and to follow Him.

You can hear Jesus' voice in various ways[1] including:

- Word of God (John 1:1-3)
- Providential workings (Psalm 136)
- Influence and impression of Holy Spirit (Hebrews 3:7-8)
- Nature (Psalm 19:1-3)

Always verify that you are following the right voice by comparing it with the Word of God.

What does it mean to be in the fold?

- I choose to leave the flocks who are on the broad way, no matter how pleasing or familiar they are to me. I choose Jesus as my Shepherd, and He knows me as His sheep.
- I choose to believe in Jesus and to put my trust and confidence in Him. Whatever He says, I believe without doubting or debating.
- I choose to become familiar with His voice. I will no longer pay attention to the many strangers, but have learned to identify His voice by experience and to listen carefully when He speaks.
- I choose to follow Jesus my Shepherd. I daily strive to imitate His example in my life and to conform my character to His.

---

1   MYP p. 156; CG p. 45

- I choose to obey Jesus out of my love for Him, encouraged that He Who kept God's commandments knows how to empower me to keep them. *"If you keep My commandments, you will abide in My love, just as I have kept My Father's commandments and abide in His love." (John 15:10)*

Further Study

John 10

Ezekiel 34

Use your Lamp

"These were more fair-minded
than those in Thessalonica,
in that they received the word with all readiness, and searched
the Scriptures daily
to find out whether these things were so."
(Acts 17:11)

One pleasant evening, my wife and I decided to take a walk outside under the stars. The moon was not up, but thousands of stars sparkled brightly in the sky. So that we could see the stars better, I turned off my flashlight and put it in my pocket.

Returning toward our hut, we took a narrow foot-path. We knew the path well and were nearly home when I felt impressed (I believe by the Holy Spirit) to pull out my light and turn it on. When I did, we stopped abruptly, for before us in the path lay a deadly sand viper. If I had not turned on my flashlight, we would not have seen the snake until it bit one or the other of us. We thanked God for the light and for saving us from danger that evening.

This experience taught us an important lesson: *Use your lamp*! My flashlight or lamp was with me, but it was useless to me as long as it was in my pocket. It was only useful to me when I pulled it out of my pocket and turned it on. The light revealed a deadly danger in our path, just before us.

Do you *use your lamp*? Unfortunately, many people do not. Some do not value the Bible enough to purchase one for themselves; they claim, "It is too expensive!" Yet the same people spend money for clothes, for food, for a telephone, and for phone credit. They spend money at the hospital to find physical health, but they don't give a second thought to their spiritual health. They spend money for tea and food and other things when a person has died, but they don't give a second thought about investing in eternal life. They will put forth amazing effort to walk many kilometers to go to the market on market day to search for some needed item, but will put little to no effort into searching for the truth. If you have no Bible at home, make a decision to save a little money and buy one as soon as you can so that you, too, can *use your lamp*.

Other people already own a Bible at home, but they see no reason to *use their lamp*. Termites nibble at the pages as it collects dust in the corner. Perhaps they dust it off once a week so they can look good walking to church with a Bible in their hands. One day a foolish girl tried to sell her Bible to us so that she could buy some oil to beautify her skin! She obviously did not understand the value of her lamp.

Your Bible is not of much value to you if you do not read it!

"Again, the kingdom of heaven is like treasure hidden in a field, which a man found and hid; and for joy over it he goes and sells all that he has and buys that field." (Matthew 13:44)

Imagine with me that you are in a very difficult situation and you see no solution. As you walk along, you get tired and decide to rest in the shade of a tree. Unknown to you, a great treasure is hidden in the ground among the roots. If only you knew about the treasure, you could dig it up and find a solution to your difficult situation. But you sit there hopelessly because you do not know the treasure that is within your reach.

In this parable,[2] the field containing treasure represents the Word of God. The treasure represents the gospel. God does not purposefully hide the treasure from us. It is people throughout the ages who have hidden the treasure. The treasure in the word of God can be hidden by:

- …traditions handed down from generation to generation.
- …human interpretations of the Scriptures.
- …taking the sayings of others as truth.
- …refusing to give up selfish, ungodly practices and habits.
- …insisting on our own preconceived ideas and opinions rather than being changed by truth.
- …placing the requirements of man above the requirements of God while searching for earthly treasure, riches, honor, power.

"But even if our gospel is veiled, it is veiled to those who are perishing, whose minds the god of this age has blinded, who do

---

2   Many thoughts in this chapter are gleaned from COL p. 104-105

not believe, lest the light of the gospel of the glory of Christ, who is the image of God, should shine on them." (2 Corinthians 4:3-4)

Are you refusing to *use your lamp*? Are you blindly refusing to let the light of truth shine on you? Are you afraid that you will be forced to give up certain traditions that are precious to you? Are you afraid that you will have to sacrifice your ungodly habits? Are you afraid that you will have to give up your position? Don't be stupid! Take the time to uncover hidden treasure in God's Word. Understand the value of eternal things compared with earthly things.

"For what profit is it to a man if he gains the whole world, and loses his own soul? Or what will a man give in exchange for his soul?" (Matthew 16:26)

Scripture knowledge is very important for our salvation. Rejecting knowledge is a very serious offense in God's sight. He has given us an opportunity to discover the immense treasure of truth, yet some of us are actually afraid to discover truth.

We will be held accountable for that which we could have known because we should have known, but we refused to know because we did not want to know.

"My people are destroyed for lack of knowledge. Because you have rejected knowledge, I also will reject you from being priest for Me; because you have forgotten the law of your God, I also will forget your children." (Hosea 4:6)

Perhaps you are among the many people who are content with a superficial understanding of the Bible.

Perhaps you feel that you already know your Bible. Perhaps you are a member who has attended church for many years and have heard many Bible verses many times. Or perhaps you are an elder or pastor and feel like you pretty much know about the Bible now. You feel like you already know the true path and can navigate it on your own without a lamp.

Remember the deadly snake in the path? You are never safe unless you *use your lamp*! Read your Bible. Study it. Dig for treasure. Do not feel safe using a few weak light beams flickering from your neighbor's lamp or even from your pastor's lamp. No matter what your age, education, experience in life, or knowledge, *use your lamp*!

How can you use your lamp?

- Search your Bible daily for treasure. If you can't read, ask a family member or friend or neighbor who can read to join you in your search.

- Never get tired of searching, thinking that you already have what is essential.

- Do not be content with a guess or speculation in regard to the truth.

- Never take the sayings of another person for truth without carefully verifying in Scripture.

Even if a very experienced, highly trained teacher or pastor is teaching you, never take his word automatically. Be like the Bereans. As they listened to Paul's teaching, they were convicted of the truth. Paul was obviously inspired of God, and even wrote a large portion of the New

Testament. Yet the people in Berea were wise and searched the Scriptures daily to verify Paul's message.

"These were more fair-minded than those in Thessalonica, in that they received the word with all readiness, and searched the Scriptures daily to find out whether these things were so."
(Acts 17:11)

Today, if people would simply *use their lamp* and verify in the Bible the teachings they hear in church, hundreds of thousands of people would discover that they are being taught error. But unfortunately, many people are not willing to be convinced that they are in error. They prefer to believe the teachings of men as the teachings of God and will actually mock the message of truth. While claiming to have light, they actually prefer darkness rather than light. They receive their light from a source other than the Bible, but it is not the true light.

"Therefore take heed that the light which is in you is not darkness. If then your whole body is full of light, having no part dark, the whole body will be full of light, as when the bright shining of a lamp gives you light." Luke 11:35-36

Do not fear to *use your lamp*. Never fear, for your Bible lamp is not like a flashlight whose batteries grow weak with time. As you search for truth and follow it, you will discover more and more truth and your light will increase with time.

"The path of the just is like the shining sun, that shines ever brighter unto the perfect day. The way of the wicked is like darkness; they do not know what makes them stumble."
(Proverbs 4:18-19)

Which path grows brighter and which path is like darkness?

The path of the just grows brighter, not the path of the disobedient. Many who desire light do not find it because of their own disobedience.

Do not be content to accept a single Bible verse that sometimes *"untaught and unstable people twist to their own destruction." (2 Peter 3:16)* Compare verses with verses to gain a more complete understanding. Let the Bible explain itself, the the Holy Spirit will be your Guide to a clearer understanding of truth.

Your salvation depends on knowing truth as it is in Jesus. Jesus is the Truth. *"And this is eternal life, that they may know You, the only true God, and Jesus Christ whom You have sent." (John 17:3)* Therefore search for it! *Use your lamp!* Use it every day. As you open your Bible, never forget to ask the the Holy Spirit to guide you into all truth, and you will discover treasures.

You do not have to know the narrow path from beginning to end. Our Good Shepherd knows that well enough. Simply follow the light that is in front of you, step by step.

"I will bring the blind by a way they did not know; I will lead them in paths they have not known. I will make darkness light before them, and crooked places straight. These things I will do for them, and not forsake them." (Isaiah 42:16)

"Ask, and it will be given to you; seek, and you will find; knock, and it will be opened to you." (Matthew 7:7)

"Yes, if you cry out for discernment, and lift up your voice for understanding, if you seek her as silver, and search for her as for hidden treasures; then you will understand the fear of the Lord, and find the knowledge of God." (Proverbs 2:3-5)

Knowing the Scriptures is very important. Yet a knowledge of Scripture is not enough to keep us safe. We must also know God. You must not only *use your lamp*, but you must trim it!

Trim your Lamp

Let your waist be girded
and your lamps burning.
(Luke 12:35)

The one and only road that is safe and secure and leads to life is a difficult road. In fact, you cannot navigate this road unless you *trim your lamp*. Keep it with you continually. It will never fail you. It will never flicker or grow dim. It will help you and guide you through even the most difficult storms of life.

In Matthew chapter 25, Jesus tells a parable[3] about ten virgins who came to meet the bridegroom, each with her lamp. All ten slept that evening while the bridegroom was delayed, but when he finally arrived at midnight, each virgin awoke to find her oil nearly finished! Only five were wise and had extra oil with them.

"And the foolish said to the wise, 'Give us some of your oil, for our lamps are going out.' But the wise answered, saying, 'No, lest there should not be enough for us and you; but go rather to those who sell, and buy for yourselves.' " (Matthew 25:8-9)

Before continuing, let's understand the meaning of the symbols.

- The bridegroom represents Jesus. (Mark 2:19-20)

---

3   Many thoughts in this chapter are gleaned from COL p. 405-421

- The virgins represent the church, who profess a pure faith. (Ephesians 5:23-27; 1 Corinthians 11:2)

- The lamp represents the Word of God. (Psalm 119:105)

- Oil represents the Holy Spirit. (Zechariah 4:2-6; Revelation 4:5)

"And while they went to buy, the bridegroom came, and those who were ready went in with him to the wedding; and the door was shut. Afterward the other virgins came also, saying, 'Lord, Lord, open to us!' But he answered and said, 'Assuredly, I say to you, I do not know you.' " (Matthew 25:10-12)

At the beginning of the parable, we cannot see a difference between the wise and the foolish. Both groups profess to know and believe only the pure light of God's Word. Both groups know their Bibles and desire to walk on the narrow path and obey the truth.

Both groups fell asleep, and both groups saw the need to *trim their lamps.* The difference was seen in preparation. The five wise virgins prepared for the night by bringing extra oil with them. The five foolish virgins discovered their need for preparation too late.

Before Jesus comes, some people will claim to become part of God's pure church. They read their Bibles, and they participate in the Bible study at church. They know that Jesus is returning soon. They even decide to be baptized to publicly declare their faith. But claiming is different than being.

But when Jesus appears to be delayed, who remains faithful?

Only those who have oil in their lamps and have been sanctified by the Holy Spirit.

Those who are not ready are those who have no oil in their lamps. They do not have the Holy Spirit. They know the theory of truth, but are not changed by it. They use their lamp, but do not *trim their lamp*. The lamp that is not trimmed and tended to may shine for a time, but it eventually grows dim and goes dark.

Without the Holy Spirit, it doesn't really matter how well you know your Bible. As you use your lamp, *trim your lamp*! In other words, ask for the Holy Spirit to teach you, not just to know the truth but to walk in the truth. He is *"the Spirit of truth"* and *"He will guide you into all truth."* *(John 16:13)* Do not be like some people who are *"...always learning and never able to come to the knowledge of the truth."* *(2 Timothy 3:7)* Allow the Holy Spirit to change your heart and to help you to practice the light and truth that you discover. Let Him destroy your old nature and give you a new heart.

The five foolish virgins accepted the Word of God much like the seed that fell on the stony ground. They are content with superficial understanding of the Scriptures. They accepted the truth and believed it, but they did not allow it into their hearts. It was nice for a while, but they grew tired of it. They did not know God or spend much time in prayer with Him.

"These likewise are the ones sown on stony ground who, when they hear the word, immediately receive it with gladness; and they have no root in themselves, and so endure only for a time. Afterward, when tribulation or persecution arises for the word's sake, immediately they stumble." (Mark 4:16-17)

"They speak to one another, everyone saying to his brother, 'Please come and hear what the word is that comes from the Lord.' So they come to you as people do, they sit before you as My people, and they hear your words, but they do not do them; for with their mouth they show much love, but their hearts pursue their own gain." (Ezekiel 33:30-31)

Which category are you in? Are you wise or foolish?

Spend some time in deep thought, and ask God to help you identify your true condition.

The foolish ones are the ones who:

- ...are content with superficial work. They do not deeply study the Scriptures for themselves.
- ...claim to be true followers of Jesus, but do not really follow Him.
- ...claim to know God, but do not spend regular quality time with Him.
- ...rely on the faith of others instead of their own.
- ...accept truth for a time, but do not abide in Jesus.
- ...know the Bible well, but are not changed by it.
- ...are controlled by their natural sinful desires.

In the time of Noah, the majority of people were foolish. They knew the truth which was clearly and faithfully preached by Noah, but they refused to allow truth to change them. They resisted the work of the Holy Spirit to change their hearts. They had an open opportunity to enter the ark. But at some point, the door was closed, and they were shut out in darkness to die. God said, *"My Spirit shall not strive with man forever." (Genesis 6:3)*

The same is true today! *"As it was in the days of Noah, so it will be also in the days of the Son of Man." (Luke 17:26)* This is a grave warning for us. Those who are foolish will be shut out in darkness to die eternal death. Only those who are wise will receive eternal life. Now, today, *"Do not grieve the Holy Spirit of God, by whom you were sealed for the day of redemption." (Ephesians 4:30) "For you were once darkness, but now you are light in the Lord. Walk as children of light (for the fruit of the Spirit is in all goodness, righteousness, and truth), finding out what is acceptable to the Lord." (Ephesians 5:8-10)*

If you have identified yourself as foolish, it is not too late to become wise! Learn to *trim your lamp* and always keep it trimmed.

If you are relying on the faith and belief of another person or a group of people, you will be bitterly disappointed when Jesus comes. We cannot safely choose our faith based on the faith of our parents, our culture, our church, our pastor. While truth can be shared from one person to another, character is not transferable from one person to another. I cannot receive the Holy Spirit for you, nor can you receive it for me. We each must receive the

Holy Spirit individually and let Him change our hearts individually. We must each believe in Jesus and have a personal faith in Him.

Here is how you can be counted among the wise who *trim their lamps:*

- Abide in Jesus. Be connected to Him. Talk with Him every day in prayer. Become acquainted with Jesus.

- Never study God's Word without first praying for the guidance of the Holy Spirit.

- Ask the Holy Spirit to change your heart and help you to truly believe. Do not rely on the belief of another person, no matter how holy or good they seem.

- Make Jesus a part of your everyday life.

- Share light with others. Your lamp not only brightens your path, but it can help others become *"wise for salvation." (2 Timothy 3:15)*

Walk in the Light!

Thus says the Lord:
"Behold, I set before you
the way of life
and the way of death."
(Jeremiah 21:8)

Today, it is not popular to *walk in the light.* The many roads are much more popular. Most people think that the narrow path is too narrow, too straight, too difficult. But Jesus sets before us only two choices. He counts the many roads as one broad path, because their common destination is death. Jesus sets before us:

- The way of life
- The way of death

That's it! Which way are you choosing today? You must choose very carefully, for this is a life and death decision.

"Thus says the Lord: 'Stand in the ways and see, and ask for the old paths, where the good way is, and walk in it; then you will find rest for your souls.' " (Jeremiah 6:16)

Noah chose to *walk in the light,* although this was certainly not popular in his day. People mocked the Word of God thinking that surely, if it were true, more people would be paying attention. In the end, only Noah and his family were saved alive in the ark. Truth triumphed.

Daniel's three friends chose to *walk in the light,* even though it certainly was not popular that day to obey God. These three men remained loyal to God and refused to participate in a system of worship set up by man. Truth triumphed.

Daniel chose to *walk in the light,* even though it was not popular to do so. The decree of false worship was universal and applied to everybody. Everybody else chose to obey the king's command. But Daniel chose to obey God's command. God saved him from the lions. Truth triumphed.

Jesus chose to *walk in the light,* even as He Himself is light. When alone and tempted, He relied on the Word of God and His Father for strength. He persevered through much persecution and hardship and even death after *"all the disciples forsook Him and fled." (Matthew 26:56)* But truth triumphed!

Countless men and women throughout the ages have chosen to walk in the light. At times, they have done so in relative peace. At other times, they have been persecuted and hunted like animals by people who hated truth. Even if a person dies for walking in the light, truth always triumphs.

Today, if you are not walking in the light, wake up! If you know truth but are not walking in truth, you are in a dangerous position. Error will not triumph! The longer you insist on walking in the broad path of error, the more difficult it will be for you to turn from this path of eternal destruction and death to the path of light and life. The more you resist the voice of the Holy Spirit guiding you into truth, the fainter His voice becomes until you may no longer hear it.

"Therefore, to him who knows to do good and does not do it, to him it is sin." (James 4:17)

"For if we sin willfully after we have received the knowledge of the truth, there no longer remains a sacrifice for sins, but a certain fearful expectation of judgment, and fiery indignation which will devour the adversaries." (Hebrews 10:26-27)

The broad path will never become the narrow path. The two paths diverge, or grow further and further apart with time. *"Evil men and impostors will grow worse and worse, deceiving and being deceived." (2 Timothy 3:13) "Sin, when it is full-grown, brings forth death" (James 1:15)*

Clearly, walking in the broad way is a fatal mistake. Why do so many professed Christians refuse to *walk in the light* even though they can have a knowledge of the truth? Why do they believe what they hear without verifying for themselves in Scripture? When God commands His people to do something, He expects obedience. His commandments are not for our amusement; they are to guide us safely in the narrow path!

"For whoever shall keep the whole law, and yet stumble in one point, he is guilty of all." (James 2:10)

"He who says, 'I know Him,' and does not keep His commandments, is a liar, and the truth is not in him." (1 John 2:4)

Maybe you are somebody who claims to know God. You read your Bible and attend church each week. You pray every day. Maybe you are an elder or pastor in your church. But if you remain disobedient to one or more of God's commands, your condition is clearly stated in God's Word: you are a guilty liar void of truth! Obeying most of the commandments is not enough. God expects complete obedience.

How may I walk in the light?

If you are wondering how you can make a decision to completely *walk in the light* that you know, do not be discouraged! The narrow way is difficult, and it is unpopular, but it is the way of life and true joy. Recognize that the way of light and the way of darkness do not mix. They are separate. You must choose one or the other.

"Do not be unequally yoked together with unbelievers. For what fellowship has righteousness with lawlessness? And what communion has light with darkness?" (2 Corinthians 6:14)

Ask God to give you the strength to leave darkness and to walk in the light. God is more than happy to answer your prayer.

Maybe you are thinking, "But what about all of my friends? What about all of my family? How can I walk this path alone without them?"

"So Jesus answered and said, 'Assuredly, I say to you, there is no one who has left house or brothers or sisters or father or mother or wife or children or lands, for My sake and the gospel's, who shall not receive a hundredfold now in this time--houses and

brothers and sisters and mothers and children and lands, with
persecutions--and in the age to come, eternal life.' "
(Mark 10:29-30)

Following Jesus involves a sacrifice that some people think is too great. They would rather enjoy their job for a few years on earth than eternal life in heaven. They would rather stay faithful to their church or pastor rather than faithful to Jesus. They love their family more than they love God. But we are told,

"Do not love the world or the things in the world. If anyone loves the world, the love of the Father is not in him." (1 John 2:15)

Friends, today is the time to abandon the broad road and become faithful to Jesus, no matter how difficult or impossible it may seem. Jesus says, *"I will never leave you nor forsake you." (Hebrews 13:5)*

"Therefore 'Come out from among them and be separate, says the Lord. Do not touch what is unclean, and I will receive you.' "
(2 Corinthians 6:17)

"The Lord... is longsuffering toward us, not willing that any should perish but that all should come to repentance. But the day of the Lord will come as a thief in the night, in which the heavens will pass away with a great noise, and the elements will melt with fervent heat; both the earth and the works that are in it will be burned up." (2 Peter 3:9-10)

"[God] desires all men to be saved and to come to the knowledge of the truth." (1 Timothy 2:4)

"And this is eternal life, that they may know You, the only true God, and Jesus Christ whom You have sent." (John 17:3)

God's desire for you is to give you eternal life. God wants you to know the truth. God wants you to know Him. Do you know Him? If not, you can learn to know Him. Do you hear His voice speaking to you today? If not, you can learn to recognize His voice. Will you decide now to follow Him?

"Today, if you will hear His voice, do not harden your hearts." (Hebrews 3:15)

Through God's power, you can choose the way of truth and life. Make God's Word your only standard, your only guide. As you do so, the Holy Spirit *"will guide you into all truth." (John 16:13)*

"Your ears shall hear a word behind you, saying, 'This is the way, walk in it,' whenever you turn to the right hand or whenever you turn to the left." (Isaiah 30:21)

Walking in the truth has been likened to running a race with perseverance and *"striving against sin." (Hebrews 12:4)* Only those who persevere through suffering and hardship win the race.

"Therefore we also, since we are surrounded by so great a cloud of witnesses, let us lay aside every weight, and the sin which so easily ensnares us, and let us run with endurance the race that is set before us." (Hebrews 12:1)

"For to this end we both labor and suffer reproach, because we trust in the living God, who is the Savior of all men, especially of those who believe." (1 Timothy 4:10)

"Fight the good fight of faith, lay hold on eternal life, to which you were also called and have confessed the good confession in the presence of many witnesses." (1 Timothy 6:12)

"And everyone who competes for the prize is temperate in all things. Now they do it to obtain a perishable crown, but we for an imperishable crown." (1 Corinthians 9:25)

"[God] is able to keep you from stumbling, and to present you faultless before the presence of His glory with exceeding joy..." (Jude 1:24)

May God give you the courage to make your decision to *walk in the light* today! May God fortify you and keep you from stumbling. May He give you perseverance to remain faithful to Him so that one day, when He returns to bring us home to Paradise, you will be found walking faithfully in the narrow path.

"Here is the patience of the saints; here are those who keep the commandments of God and the faith of Jesus." (Revelation 14:12)

"Be faithful until death, and I will give you the crown of life." (Revelation 2:10)

"But thanks be to God, who gives us the victory through our Lord Jesus Christ." (1 Corinthians 15:57)

My Choice

I have set before you
life and death,
blessing and cursing;
therefore choose life,
that both you and your descendants may live.
(Deuteronomy 30:19)

Please prayerfully take some time to think about the following commitments. If one point is especially difficult for you, read again the corresponding chapter in this little book.

By God's grace, and through His power, I make the following decisions today.

☐ I understand that the Bible is a *lamp for our journey*. Today, I choose to appreciate it as God's letter to me.

☐ I understand that there are *many roads* that seem right to us, but the end is death. Today, I choose to search for the road that leads to eternal life.

☐ I understand that although the *broad path* is popular, it leads to destruction. Today, I choose to not follow popular opinion or the majority as my guide.

☐ I understand that many *smooth teachers* hide the truth and are not worthy of my confidence. Today, I choose to search the Scriptures myself to verify any teaching that I hear.

68

☐ I understand that many people have *itching ears* and do not desire to know the truth because it makes them uncomfortable. Today, I choose to listen carefully to the truth and to understand it.

☐ I understand that the *narrow path* is difficult and few people find it, because they insist on clinging to their own traditions and opinions. Today, I choose to completely abandon my own ideas and commit to obedience to all truth that I discover.

☐ I understand that the only way to stay in the narrow way is to be *in Jesus*. Today, I choose to abide in Him and to let Him abide in me. I choose to spend time talking with Him in prayer and reading His Word every day.

☐ I understand that Jesus has *other sheep* that are not yet in the fold. Today, I choose to be one of Jesus sheep in His fold by believing in Him, listening to His voice, and following Him. I also choose to share my light with the other sheep and invite them into the fold.

☐ I understand that my lamp is not useful unless I *use my lamp*. Today, I choose to faithfully read and study my Bible, not at a surface level, but with a goal of understanding truth.

☐ I understand that if I do not *trim my lamp*, I will not be ready for Jesus' soon return. Today, I choose to always ask for the Holy Spirit before I read and study my Bible, and I choose to allow Him to change my heart so that I will not only profess, but practice the truth.

☐ I understand that it is unpopular to *walk in the light.* Today, I choose to obey all truth that I discover in God's Word and to reject all false teaching.

May God bless you,

may Jesus be your Example,

and may the Holy Spirit sanctify you

as you faithfully walk the narrow path!

As you have read this book

and have asked yourself the question

"Which road next?"

may you be able to say with me today,

"I have chosen

the way

of truth."
(Psalm 119:30)

Desert Tree Ministry

http://deserttreeministry.org

(BK0007-ENG_Which-Road-Next_createspace.odt) 2017